Ready for

College English

A Culture-Specific Reading & Grammar Book

Authors Myeong-Hee Seong · Yoon-Hee Shin · Jennifer Doh
Editor Lyle A. Lewin

지식인

Profile

Myeong-Hee Seong
Ph.D. in English Education, Korea Univ.
Professor, Eulji University

Yoon-Hee Shin
M.A. California State University, Fullerton

Jennifer Doh
Professor, Eulji University

Editor
Lyle A. Lewin
Professor, Eulji University

Ready for College English
A Culture-Specific Reading & Grammar Book

2014년 12월 26일 초판 1쇄 발행
2024년 3월 1일 초판 7쇄 발행

지은이 | Myeong-Hee Seong · Yoon-Hee Shin · Jennifer Doh
펴낸이 | 김종욱 · 명사동
펴낸곳 | 지식인
등 록 | 제301-2013-134호
주 소 | 서울시 도봉구 도봉로 180길 20 투웨니퍼스트 102동 602호
전 화 | 02)2266-8606
팩 스 | 02)2266-8607
E-mail | jisikin2013@naver.com

ISBN 978-89-98591-37-3 (93740)

값 13,000원

Ready for
College English

Table of Contents

Ready for
College English

UNIT 01

Potluck

TOPIC READING

Read about Potluck.

A potluck is a party where each person, or group, brings one dish of food to be shared with everyone. Other names for this are: potluck dinner, faith supper, shared lunch, or bring-a-plate. It **is also referred to** as a smorgasbord or potlatch. The word potluck was first seen in the 16th century England, from the writer, Thomas Nashe. It originally meant "food provided for an unexpected or uninvited guest; the luck of the pot". The modern meaning of a "shared meal, where guests bring their own food" has been around since the late 19th century or early 20th century. To Irish people, a potluck was a meal with no particular menu. Everyone participating brought a dish for all to share. The term **comes from** a time when groups of Irish women got together and cooked dinner for their families. They would only use one cooking dish called a "pot" and they cooked one meal using whatever food they **happened to** have that day.

Potluck dinners are often organized by community groups. The only traditional rule is that each dish should be large enough to be shared by a good portion, but not necessarily all, of the expected guests. In many cases each person agrees, before the party, to bring a certain thing. This way, there are a variety of things, and not a lot of one thing. Guests may bring any form of food, **ranging from** the main course **to** desserts. In the United States, potlucks **are associated with** slow-cooker dishes, casseroles, dessert bars and salads. Potluck style is getting popular as a way to entertain guests because it lowers the cost of having a party. Potluck dinners, brunches, and potluck wedding receptions are being hosted as alternatives to traditional catered events.

READING COMPREHENSION

Answer the questions based on the story above.

1. What is a potluck?

2. Have you ever been to a potluck? Is it a good idea? Why?

3. When did the word potluck appear according to the story?

4. What is the only traditional rule for potlucks?

5. Are potluck meals gaining popularity? If so, why?

KEY EXPRESSIONS

Write the sentences in English using the words or phrases given.

1. be referred to as

   ex) It is also referred to as a smorgasbord or potlatch.

   1) ______________________________

   2) ______________________________

2. come from

   ex) The term comes from a time when groups of Irish women got together and cooked dinner for their families.

   1) ______________________________

   2) ______________________________

3. happen to

   ex) They cooked one meal with whatever food they happened to have that day.

   1) ______________________________

   2) ______________________________

4. range from A to B

   ex) Guests may bring in any form of food, ranging from the main course to desserts.

   1) ______________________________

   2) ______________________________

5. be associated with

   ex) In the United States, potlucks are associated with slow-cooker dishes, casseroles, dessert bars and salads.

   1) ______________________________

   2) ______________________________

MAKING SENTENCES

Unscramble the words to make the sentences.

1. one of the most popular places / is referred to as / Jeju Island / in the world

   Jeju Island ______________________________________.

2. this Friday / am going shopping / with my friend / I

   I ______________________________________.

3. come from / Where / our English teacher / does

   Where ______________________________________?

4. every three months / goes to the movies / with his wife / He / once

   He ______________________________________.

5. her friend / She / on her way to school / happened to meet

   She ______________________________________.

6. collected money, / counted it / they / they / After

   After ______________________________________.

7. The temperatures / in Seoul / range from 30℃ / in summer / to 35℃

   The temperatures ______________________________________.

8. his fault / admitted / The sales person / that it was

   The sales person ______________________________________.

9. We / with each other / sometimes / when we communicate / use body languages

We ____.

10. I / those kinds of people / be associated with / don't want to

I ____.

GRAMMAR FOCUS

Choose the correct noun in parentheses.

1. (The man, A man, Man) in my class has two sons and one daughter.

2. I think the woman in the red dress is (an American, the American, a American).

3. The man singing on the stage is my (manager, management, manage).

4. One of my students gave me (a flower, the flower, a flowers) on May, 15th.

5. The couple next to my house has (three cats, the three cats, three cat).

6. My neighbors called (a man, the man, the men) wearing a red tie "Tom".

7. When I arrive at work, I always have (a cups of coffee, the cup of coffee, a cup of coffee).

8. There are (many customs, much customs, a lot of custom) in Korea just like other countries.

9. My boss made (a surprising announcement, an surprising announcement, a surprising announce) about the project after the meeting.

10. I will be (a English teacher, the English teacher, an English teacher) after graduating.

FURTHER PRACTICE

Choose the one word or phrase that best completes the sentence.

1. ____________ in the conference should register one week in advance.
   - a) All participation
   - b) All participate
   - c) All participants
   - d) All participating

2. The police gave me ____________ about the car accident.
   - a) an information
   - b) some information
   - c) some informations
   - d) a lot of informations

3. During her ____________, she mentioned her new book about the history of Mexico.
   - a) speech
   - b) speaking
   - c) speak
   - d) spoke

4. It took ____________ hour and ____________ half for them to finish the project.
   - a) a — a
   - b) a — an
   - c) an — an
   - d) an — a

5. According to the bill, not only calls, but repeated ____________ will also be prohibited.
   - a) the e-mail
   - b) an e-mail
   - c) e-mails
   - d) e-mail

6. Several companies have not decided ____________ the meeting or not.
   - a) whether attending
   - b) whether to attend
   - c) whether to attended
   - d) whether being attend

7. It's obvious that North Korea is trying to test the ___________ of South Korea.

a) paternality b) patent
c) patience d) patient

8. My aunt bought me some ___________ for my birthday present last week.

a) books b) book
c) a book d) the books

9. ___________ in his room is very nice and quite new.

a) A furniture b) The furniture
c) The furnitures d) Furnitures

10. My nephew in the United States became ___________ with a love of literature.

a) a scientist b) a science
c) science d) scientist

Ready for
College English

UNIT 02

Black Friday

TOPIC READING

Read about Black Friday.

Black Friday is the day after Thanksgiving Day (the fourth Thursday of November) in the United States. It **is often regarded** as the beginning of the Christmas shopping season. In recent years, most major stores open extremely early and offer big discounts to **kick off** the holiday shopping season. It **is similar to** Boxing Day in Canada. However, Black Friday is not a holiday. California and some other states observe "The Day After Thanksgiving" as a holiday for state government employees. This is often **in lieu of** another federal holiday **such as** Columbus Day. Many non-retail employees and schools have both Thanksgiving and the day after off, followed by a weekend; this increases the number of potential shoppers. It has been the busiest shopping day of the year since 2005.

The name 'Black Friday' originated in Philadelphia. It originally described the heavy and disruptive traffic which would occur on the day after Thanksgiving. Use of the term became popular outside of Philadelphia around 1975. Later a new meaning was given for the name: retailers normally lost money, known as "in the red" from January through November. However, "Black Friday" is the day that many businesses begin to make money, known as "in the black."

For many years, it was common for retailers to open at 6:00 a.m., but in the late 2000s many opened at 5:00 or even 4:00. This was taken to a new extreme in 2011, when several retailers, including Target, Kohl's, Macy's, and Best Buy, opened at midnight for the first time. In 2012, Walmart and several others opened most of their stores at 8:00 p.m. on Thanksgiving Day, except in places where it is illegal. This made many workers angry and caused them to walk out of work.

READING COMPREHENSION

Answer the questions based on the story above.

1. What is Black Friday? When does it take place?

2. According to the reading, what is the modern meaning of "Black Friday?"

3. Why do so many people shop on Black Friday?

4. What do the phrases "in the red" and "in the black" mean?

5. Retailers are opening earlier every year. Do workers like this? Why or why not?

KEY EXPRESSIONS

Write the sentences in English using the words or phrases given.

1. be regarded as

   ex) It is often regarded as the beginning of the Christmas shopping season.

   1) ______

   2) ______

2. kick off

   ex) In recent years, most major stores open extremely early and offer big discounts to kick off the holiday shopping season.

   1) ______

   2) ______

3. be similar to

   ex) It is similar to Boxing Day in Canada.

   1) ______

   2) ______

4. in lieu of

   ex) This is often in lieu of another federal holiday such as Columbus Day.

   1) ______

   2) ______

5. such as

   ex) This is often in lieu of another federal holiday such as Columbus Day.

   1) ______

   2) ______

MAKING SENTENCES

Unscramble the words to make the sentences.

1. on the market / is regarded as / This smart phone / one of the best ones

   This smart phone ______________________________________.

2. on Sept, 19 / kicked off / The Incheon Asian Games

   The Incheon Asian games ______________________________________.

3. yours / exactly / My opinion / is similar to

   My opinion ______________________________________.

4. is sentenced to / In lieu of / Tom / jail term, / community service

   In lieu of ______________________________________.

5. like fruits / I / and bananas / oranges, / apples, / such as

   I ______________________________________.

6. the rural areas / Some students / are from / in my class

   Some students ______________________________________.

7. in this city / have you been / How long

   How long ______________________________________?

8. had already finished / told me / that he / his homework / He

   He ______________________________________.

9. in the park / are sitting / Most people / on the bench

Most people ____.

10. phone number / your name / Can I have / please / and

Can I have ____?

GRAMMAR FOCUS

Choose the correct pronoun in parentheses.

1. My brother has lost his cell phone, so he is using (me, mine, my).

2. Suzan cut (herself, hers, her) finger while she was cooking this morning.

3. My daughter went shopping with some friends of (hers, her, she) yesterday.

4. There are two balls in the box; (one, the other, another) is red and (one, the other, another) is green.

5. Kim and Lee are looking at (them, theirs, themselves) in the mirror.

6. The manager from the head office asked (I, me, myself) to finish the project as soon as possible.

7. No one knows when (our, we, us) delivery of fresh flowers will arrive at the office.

8. My husband bought (I, my, me) some flowers for my birthday. (They, Their, Them) were gorgeous.

9. My boss made some mistakes and (they, them, themselves) caused (his, he, him) resignation.

10. My sister and I ordered cell-phones on the internet a week ago. (Her, She, Hers) has already arrived, but (mine, my, me) hasn't.

FURTHER PRACTICE

Choose the one word or phrase that best completes the sentence.

1. I heard ____________ singing at the party last night.
   - a) Mary and she's sister
   - b) Mary and her sister
   - c) Mary and hers sister
   - d) Mary and her's sister

2. Everybody in my class knows the relationship between ____________ is very close.
   - a) you and him
   - b) you and he
   - c) you and his
   - d) you and his's

3. The blue pants in John's room are ____________.
   - a) my
   - b) me
   - c) mine
   - d) myself

4. The families of the victims of the ferry tragedy called for the committee to indict ____________ responsible for the incident.
   - a) that
   - b) those
   - c) this
   - d) these

5. ____________ takes the abandoned pets to the abandoned pet care center because she / he knows what will happen to the animals there.
   - a) Not no one
   - b) Not everyone
   - c) An one
   - d) Each one

6. This shirt is too small for me. Do you have any larger ____________?
   - a) the others
   - b) another
   - c) others
   - d) ones

7. The cost of living in New York is higher than ____________ in Seoul.

a) that
b) those
c) this
d) those

8. ____________ unusual for a former presidential candidate to take face indictment.

a) There is
b) It is
c) These are
d) Those are

9. He is ____________ of the richest people in the world.

a) one
b) any
c) ones
d) each

10. There are twenty female students in my department. Some of them have long hair but ____________ have short hair.

a) the others
b) anothers
c) others
d) other

Ready for
College English

UNIT 03

Baby Showers

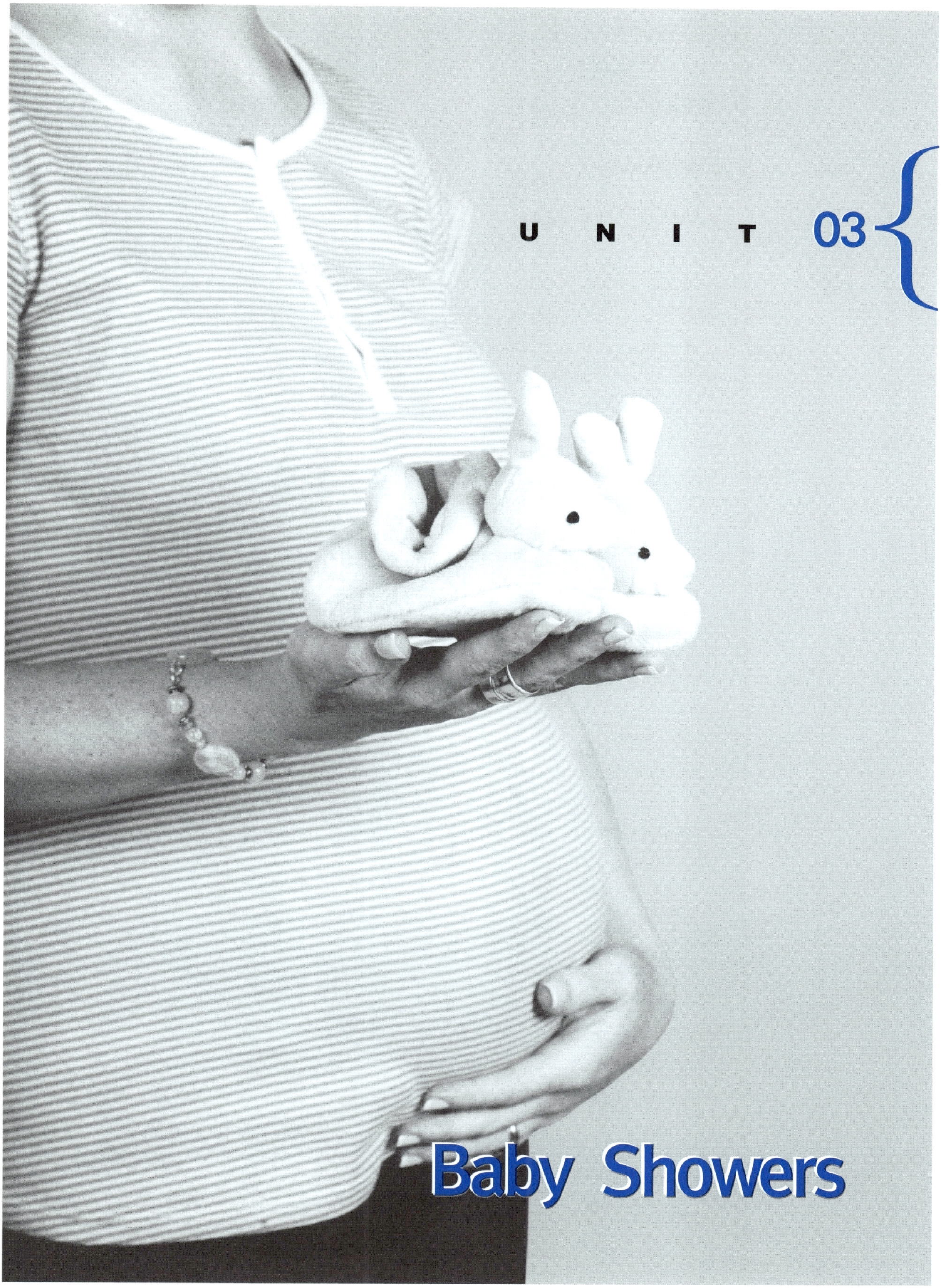

TOPIC READING

Read about Baby Showers.

In some countries, a baby shower is a way to celebrate the pending or recent birth of a child. People present gifts to the mother at a party. The word, shower means that the expectant mother is "showered" with gifts. Traditionally, baby showers were given only for the family's first child and only women were invited. The original intent was for women to share wisdom and lessons on the art of becoming a mother. Over time, **it** has become common **to** hold them for subsequent, or adopted children. **It** is not uncommon **for** a mother **to** have more than one baby shower, such as one with friends and another with co-workers.

According to etiquette authority, Miss Manners, since the party centers on gift-giving, the baby shower is typically arranged and hosted by a close friend rather than a member of the family. It is considered rude for families to beg for gifts **on behalf of** their members. However, this custom varies by culture or region. In some, it is expected and customary for a close female family member to host the baby shower, often the baby's grandmother. Most hosts invite only women to baby showers, although there is no firm rule requiring this. If the shower **is held** after the baby's birth, then the baby is usually brought to the party. Showers typically include food but not a full meal. Guests bring small gifts for the mother. Typical gifts include diapers, blankets, baby bottles, clothes, and toys. It is common to open the gifts during the party.

READING COMPREHENSION

Answer the questions based on the story above.

1. What is a baby shower?

2. Have you been to a baby shower?

3. What are the good points about having a baby shower?

4. Would you have a baby shower? Why or why not?

5. Do you think men should be invited to a baby shower? Why or why not?

KEY EXPRESSIONS

Write the sentences in English using the words or phrases given.

1. It ~ to Verb

ex) It has become common to hold them for subsequent or adopted children.

1) ______________________________

2) ______________________________

2. It ~ for ~ to Verb

ex) It is not uncommon for a parent to have more than one baby shower.

1) ______________________________

2) ______________________________

3. According to

ex) According to etiquette authority, Miss Manner, since the party centers on gift-giving, the baby shower is typically arranged and hosted by a close friend.

1) ______________________________

2) ______________________________

4. on behalf of

ex) It is considered rude for families to beg for gifts on behalf of their members.

1) ______________________________

2) ______________________________

5. be held

ex) If the shower is held after the baby's birth, then the baby is usually brought to the party.

1) ______________________________

2) ______________________________

MAKING SENTENCES

Unscramble the words to make the sentences.

1. in the store / goods / A variety of / are displayed

   A variety of ____.

2. are round / The roofs / of the temples

   The roofs ____.

3. their meal / in the restaurant / Many people / and / are having / talking

   Many people ____.

4. is important / a good job / to study / to get / It / hard

   It ____.

5. yesterday / Who took / to the hospital / your mother

   Who took ____?

6. shirt / The woman / a short-sleeved / is wearing

   The woman ____.

7. will be held / next month / The event / at the school

   The event ____.

8. on behalf of / am speaking / I / my family

   I ____.

9. the problem / for us / in just five minutes / is impossible / to solve / It

It ____.

10. three people / According to / were killed / the newspaper, / in the accident

According to ____.

GRAMMAR FOCUS

Choose the correct verb form and tense in parentheses.

1. Every Sunday she (played, play, plays) tennis with her friend.

2. He read books and (studied, study, studying) in the library last night.

3. When I saw her on the street, she (was waiting, was wait, has waited) for her son.

4. I sometimes (work, works, worked) from 8 a.m. to 9 p.m.

5. Haven't you (hear, had heard, heard) his new song yet?

6. I (go, have been, went) to Jeju Island three times so far.

7. She (graduated, graduate, has graduated) from the university in 2010.

8. When I arrived at the station, the train (had already left, has already left, have left).

9. As soon as you (hear, hears, heard) the bell, you have to leave the classroom.

10. While I (was walking, am walking, was walked) along the street last Friday, I (seen, see, saw) Mr. Kim with his girl friend.

FURTHER PRACTICE

Choose the one word or phrase that best completes the sentence.

1. He usually ____________ to school by subway, but he ____________ to school by bus tomorrow.
   a) goes — is going
   b) goes — goes
   c) go — is going
   d) is going — goes

2. Prosecutors ____________ two days ago to take five lawmakers into custody at the National Assembly.
   a) attempt
   b) have attempted
   c) attempts
   d) attempted

3. North Korea ____________ for the resumption of negotiations since the last meeting in late 2008.
   a) called
   b) call
   c) has called
   d) calls

4. The meeting ____________ from 9:30 a.m. to 12:30 p.m. tomorrow.
   a) runs
   b) will run
   c) run
   d) ran

5. Fifty-six foreigners from nine countries ____________ from Korea over the past five years.
   a) have been deported
   b) have deported
   c) has been deported
   d) had been deported

6. The lawmaker ____________ to call in two CEOs of foreign pharmaceutical companies as witnesses.
   a) is preparing
   b) prepare
   c) preparing
   d) had prepared

7. Since the September 11, terrorist attacks on the World Trade Center, major countries ____________ new laws on handling terrorists and preventing attacks.

a) passed
b) has passed
c) had passed
d) have passed

8. When he ____________ the paper, I will check whether there are mistakes or not.

a) will finish
b) finishes
c) finished
d) finish

9. The woman claimed that she ____________ a ghost before.

a) saw
b) see
c) had seen
d) has seen

10. My husband used to ____________ computer science at a university in Seoul.

a) teaching
b) teach
c) taught
d) be taught

Ready for
College English

UNIT 04

La Tomatina

TOPIC READING

Read about La Tomatina.

La Tomatina is a festival that is held in the Valencian town of Bunol. Participants throw tomatoes and **get involved in** this tomato fight just for fun during the festival. It is held on the last Wednesday of August, during the week of festivities of Bunol. In 1945, some woodland animals were eating all the watermelons during the parade of the "Little Rabbit". The people at the parade threw tomatoes at the animals; one missed and hit a person. Then, they started throwing the tomatoes and the police had to arrest everyone.

The following year the young people repeated the fight on the same Wednesday of August. This time they brought their own tomatoes from home. They were again scattered by the police. After repeating this in subsequent years, the tradition was established. In 1950, the town **allowed** the tomato hurl **to** take place. However, the next year it was again stopped. A lot of young people were imprisoned but the Bunol residents **forced** the authorities **to** let them go. The festival gained popularity with more and more participants getting involved every year. After subsequent years it was banned again with threats of serious penalties. Considering the popularity of the festival and the alarming demand, the festival became official with certain rules and restrictions in 1957. These rules have **gone through** a lot of modifications over the years. In 1980, the town hall took the responsibility of organizing the festival.

READING COMPREHENSION

Answer the questions based on the story above.

1. What is La Tomatina?

2. Why do you think La Tomatina was banned several times?

3. Do you want to go to La Tomatina? Why or why not?

4. Do you have anything similar to La Tomatina in your culture?

5. What are the good points and bad points of La Tomatina?

KEY EXPRESSIONS

Write the sentences in English using the words or phrases given.

1. get involved in

   ex) Participants throw tomatoes and get involved in this tomato fight just for fun.

   1) ______________________________

   2) ______________________________

2. allow Object to Verb

   ex) In 1950, the town allowed the tomato hurl to take place.

   1) ______________________________

   2) ______________________________

3, force Object to Verb

   ex) A lot of young people were imprisoned but the Bunol residents forced the authorities to let them go.

   1) ______________________________

   2) ______________________________

4. go through

   ex) These rules have gone through a lot of modifications over the years.

   1) ______________________________

   2) ______________________________

5. take the responsibility of

   ex) In 1980, the town hall took the responsibility of organizing the festival.

   1) ______________________________

   2) ______________________________

MAKING SENTENCES

Unscramble the words to make the sentences.

1. get involved in / wouldn't like to / it / I

   I ____.

2. take responsibility for / of him / should / the death / You

   You ____.

3. about the accident / The police / to tell / forced / the truth / him

   The police ____.

4. to watch / her children / allows / educational programs / She

   She ____.

5. many difficult times / People / in their lives / go through

   People ____.

6. anytime / can return / You / faulty products

   You ____.

7. so hot that / The dish / I / it / was / couldn't eat

   The dish ____.

8. she / late / My sister / was sick / went to school / because

   My sister ____.

9. your essay / I / anything interesting / didn't find / in

I ____.

10. very well / cooks / My mother-in-law / food

My mother-in-law ______________________________.

GRAMMAR FOCUS

Circle the subject and choose the correct verb form in parentheses.

1. The number of books on my desk (is / are / were) ten.

2. A number of students (is / are / was) in my class.

3. There (is / are / was) two books in my backpack.

4. Two-thirds of my classmates (is / are / was) from Korea.

5. The book about the history of America (is / are / were) interesting.

6. Every (chair / chairs / chair's) at the restaurant (is / are / were) taken.

7. The customers at the table (is / are / was) talking each other.

8. Each of my friends (like / likes) Italian food.

9. Seven hours of sleep each night (is / was / are) enough for me.

10. Mathematics (is / are / were) one of the most difficult subjects.

FURTHER PRACTICE

Choose the one word or phrase that best completes the sentence.

1. Many people around the world ____________ having coffee.
   a) enjoy b) enjoyed
   c) enjoys d) is enjoying

2. Most of the tourists on this trip ____________.
   a) is Chinese b) are Chinese
   c) are Chineses d) are China people

3. The total profits ____________ over the past three years after adopting a cost-effective management system.
   a) has been increased b) has increased
   c) have increased d) have been increased

4. The price hikes, following rising commodities prices, ____________ consumers.
   a) is affecting b) will affecting
   c) are affecting d) are going to affecting

5. Neither she nor I ____________ to the party tonight.
   a) be going b) am going
   c) is going d) are going

6. Here ____________ some information for improving your English skill.
   a) are b) is
   c) has d) have

7. More than half of the newly built houses in the country ___________ Korea's heating system, ondol.

a) are adopting
b) is adopting
c) has adopted
d) adopting

8. He said his grudge against his former girlfriend of five years ___________ him to murder.

a) drives
b) drive
c) be driven
d) drove

9. My classmates, as well as I, ___________ satisfied with the test results.

a) are not
b) am not
c) is not
d) was not

10. "There ___________ noticeable problems during the construction", a company official said.

a) were not any
b) were not some
c) was not any
d) was not some

UNIT 05

The Water Festival

TOPIC READING

Read about the Water Festival.

The water festival is a New Year's celebration in Southeast Asian countries such as Burma, Cambodia, Laos, and Thailand, as well as, China. It is called the 'Water Festival' by westerners because people splash water at one another. This is a cleansing ritual to welcome the new year. Traditionally, people gently sprinkled water on **one another** as a sign of respect. As the new year falls during the hottest month in South East Asia, many people **end up** dous**ing** strangers and passersby in vehicles to show blessings and good wishes. It is believed that during this water festival, everything old must **be thrown away**, or it will bring the owner bad luck.

The festival lasts for three days. On the first day, a grand celebration marks **the beginning of** the festival. An out-door market is set up, where locals go for New Year's shopping. It is also a great place for travelers to buy local foods, snacks, and souvenirs. At night, people float river lanterns which is an old tradition in China. It is still preserved in many cities and people think that this practice drives bad luck away and brings good luck.

The climax of the festival is water splashing. For this, local people **put on** their newest and best clothes, then gather in the local Buddhist temple. People move a Buddhist statue to the courtyard, and then it is splashed with water. This important ritual is called 'Bathing Buddha'. The completion of the 'Bathing Buddha' ritual is mutual water splashing among people. Accordingly, people flock to the streets with pots, pans, bottles, or whatever, and they enjoy splashing water on one another freely without any restrictions.

READING COMPREHENSION

Answer the questions based on the story above.

1. What is the water festival?

2. What is the meaning of splashing water on one another?

3. What is the 'Bathing Buddha' ritual?

4. Do you think it would be fun to have this kind of water festival in your country? Why or why not?

5. Would you take part in this kind of water festival as a traveler? Why or why not?

KEY EXPRESSIONS

Write the sentences in English using the words or phrases given.

1. one another

   ex) Traditionally people gently sprinkled water on one another as a sign of respect.

   1) ______________________________

   2) ______________________________

2. end up ~ing

   ex) Many people end up dousing strangers and passersby in vehicles to show blessings and good wishes.

   1) ______________________________

   2) ______________________________

3. throw away

   ex) It is believed that during this water festival, everything old must be thrown away, or it will bring the owner bad luck.

   1) ______________________________

   2) ______________________________

4. the beginning of

   ex) On the first day, a grand celebration marks the beginning of the festival.

   1) ______________________________

   2) ______________________________

5. put on

   ex) For this, local people put on their newest and best clothes, then gather in the local Buddhist temple.

   1) ______________________________

   2) ______________________________

MAKING SENTENCES

Unscramble the words to make the sentences.

1. a sleeping baby / She / in her room / is looking at

   She ____.

2. the broken window / He / has already thrown away

   He ____.

3. the test / Unfortunately / ended up failing / he

   Unfortunately, ______________________________________.

4. and I / one another / are so different from / My sister

   My sister ____.

5. out of the house / He / and / put on / rushed / a black suit

   He ____.

6. this year / FTA / at the beginning of / will take effect

   FTA ____.

7. was bored / was boring / and / The movie / I

   The movie ____.

8. by my secretary / I / typed / the letter / have

   I ____.

9. waiting for / Some applicants / the job interview / are nervous

Some applicants ____.

10. the clerk / the returned item / I / gave / to

I ____.

GRAMMAR FOCUS

Choose the correct adjective or adverb in parentheses.

1. This red scarf matches your dress (perfectly, perfect, perfection).

2. Playing tennis every day keeps me (health, healthy, healthful).

3. The food on the table smells (well, better, good).

4. She speaks English very (well, good, better) and has very (well, good, better) pronunciation.

5. My daughter gave me a (beautifully, beauty, beautiful) necklace.

6. She speaks (loudly, loud, loudness) and everyone can hear it.

7. (Little, Few, A little) employees are late to the meeting.

8. It is (high like, highly like, highly likely) that the talks will be held in early September.

9. How (many, much, any) coffee do you drink a day?

10. Her grandson makes her (happiness, happily, happy).

FURTHER PRACTICE

Choose the one word or phrase that best completes the sentence.

1. I learned that ASEAN (The Association of Southeast Asian Nations) countries are ____________ to Korea in many fields like politics and economics.
   a) importance b) important
   c) importantly d) import

2. He is less ____________ to accept her proposal.
   a) likely b) like
   c) likeness d) liken

3. We are planning to focus on how to boost our ____________ partnership in the meeting.
   a) strategy b) strategic
   c) strategically d) straight

4. It's ____________ to listen ____________ to the opinions of those concerned.
   a) advice — careful b) advisable — careful
   c) advisable — carefully d) advise — carefully

5. A growing number of people buy goods from foreign websites ____________.
   a) direct b) director
   c) directly d) directive

6. The government will expand financial support on ____________ cars.
   a) environmentally — friendly b) environmental — friendly
   c) environmentally — friend d) environmental — friend

7. ___________ 60 drug distributors have gone bankrupt since 2011.

a) Almost
b) Most
c) Nearly
d) Much

8. Visitors will also be ___________ to apply for their visas ___________ ahead of their arrival.

a) eligibly — electronically
b) eligible — electronically
c) eligible — electronic
d) eligible — electron

9. The news about the Sewol ferry disaster made me ___________.

a) sadness
b) saddle
c) sad
d) sadly

10. You can get a ___________ discount if you sign up now.

a) consider
b) considerable
c) considerate
d) consolidate

UNIT 06

Valentine's Day

TOPIC READING

Read about Valentine's Day.

Valentine's Day, also **known as** Saint Valentine's Day, is celebrated on February 14th in many countries around the world. It is a festival of romantic love and many people give cards, letters, flowers or presents to their spouse, partner, boyfriend or girlfriend. However, it is not a public holiday in most countries. Government offices, stores, schools and other organizations are open as usual.

There are **a number of** Saints called Valentine who are honored on February 14h. The day became associated with romantic love in the Middle Ages in England. The most common Valentine's Day symbols are hearts, red roses, and Cupid. Cupid is usually **portrayed as** a small winged figure with a bow and arrow. In mythology, he uses his arrow to strike the hearts of people. People who have **fallen in love** are sometimes said to have been struck by Cupid's arrow.

In the United States, couples often give presents to each other and they may arrange a romantic meal in a restaurant. Many restaurants and hotels have special offers at this time. Restaurants may be busier than usual as many people **go out** for an evening with their spouse or partner. Also, people who would like to have a romantic relationship with somebody may use this occasion. Common Valentine's Day gifts are flowers, chocolates, champagne or sparkling wine.

READING COMPREHENSION

Answer the questions based on the story above.

1. What do people do on Valentine's Day?

2. What does "to be struck by Cupid's arrow" mean?

3. What do you think about giving presents to someone you love on Valentine's Day?

4. Do you celebrate Valentine's Day in your culture? How is it different from the one in the United States?

5. As for usual dates, who pays more, men or women? What is your personal opinion on that?

KEY EXPRESSIONS

Write the sentences in English using the words or phrases given.

1. be known as

ex) *Valentine's Day, also known as Saint Valentine's Day, is celebrated on February 14th in many countries around the world.*

1) ______________________________

2) ______________________________

2. a number of

ex) *There are a number of Saints called Valentine who are honored on February 14th.*

1) ______________________________

2) ______________________________

3. be portrayed as

ex) *Cupid is usually portrayed as a small winged figure with a bow and arrow.*

1) ______________________________

2) ______________________________

4. fall in love

ex) *People who have fallen in love are sometimes said to have been struck by cupid's arrow.*

1) ______________________________

2) ______________________________

5. go out for

ex) *Restaurants may be busier than usual as many people go out for an evening with their spouse or partner.*

1) ______________________________

2) ______________________________

MAKING SENTENCES

Unscramble the words to make the sentences.

1. questions and comments / contact us / if you / have / Please / any

   Please ______________________________________.

2. go out for / dinner / next week / Why don't we / sometime

   Why don't we ______________________________________?

3. last year / and / fell in love, / They / married / met,

   They ______________________________________.

4. very much / likes / Every student / the class

   Every student ______________________________________.

5. a time of / is known as / Valentine's Day / love

   Valentine's Day ______________________________________.

6. of this course / provide you / is to / The goal / with a practical experience

   The goal ______________________________________.

7. an actor / was known as / a singer / not / The man

   The man ______________________________________.

8. in the classroom / are waiting for / A number of / their teacher / students

   A number of ______________________________________.

9. in the box / The man / something / is looking for

The man ____.

10. in the film / He / a monster / was portrayed as

He ____.

GRAMMAR FOCUS

Choose the correct participle in parentheses.

1. (Retired, Retiring, Retire) people find few places to invest and they are spending less.

2. In (advance, advanced, advancement) countries, banks do not offer high rates.

3. Two (contrasted, contrast, contrasting) scenes Tuesday showed how divided the nation is.

4. Many corporations are moving their plants to (developing, developed, develop) countries because of cheaper labor costs.

5. The (arrived, arriving, arrive) passengers had to spend an hour or more lining up for passport control and baggage inspection.

6. The (organized, organizing, organize) committee sent a two-page letter to the North.

7. The two Koreas held a (work-level, worked-level, working-level) meeting at Panmunjom in July.

8. The move is the latest in a series of efforts to make South Korea a safe country (followed, follow, following) April's ferry sinking.

9. The Seoul Central District Prosecutor's Office has (secure, securing, secured) evidence.

10. His (deteriorating, deteriorated, deteriorate) health also influenced his decision.

FURTHER PRACTICE

Choose the one word or phrase that best completes the sentence.

1. I will actively fight the accusations ____________ against me.
   a) charge b) charged
   c) charging d) chargeable

2. Asiana Airlines is paying more attention to the ____________ number of foreign visitors seeking to receive healthcare and medical service here.
   a) growing b) growed
   c) grow d) growth

3. She will take a 10-week ____________ course before being commissioned.
   a) train b) trained
   c) trainer d) training

4. Demand for coins ____________ the pope's recent visit to Korea is exceptionally high.
   a) honor b) honored
   c) honoring d) honorable

5. You are not obligated to attend the ____________ itinerary.
   a) changed b) change
   c) changing d) changer

6. The Seoul International Hiking Club has organized some special hiking in a ____________ area.
   a) restricting b) restricted
   c) restrict d) restraint

7. The Asiad and Olympics also use different ___________ procedures for medalists.

a) fundamental b) funding
c) fundraising d) fundraiser

8. He is at the center of an ___________ political controversy.

a) escalate b) escalating
c) escalated d) escalator

9. The ___________ content did not address their concerns.

a) proposed b) propose
c) proposing d) proposition

10. I was deeply ___________ by your ___________ play.

a) impressed — impressing b) impressing — impressed
c) impressed — impressed d) impressing — impressing

Ready for
College English

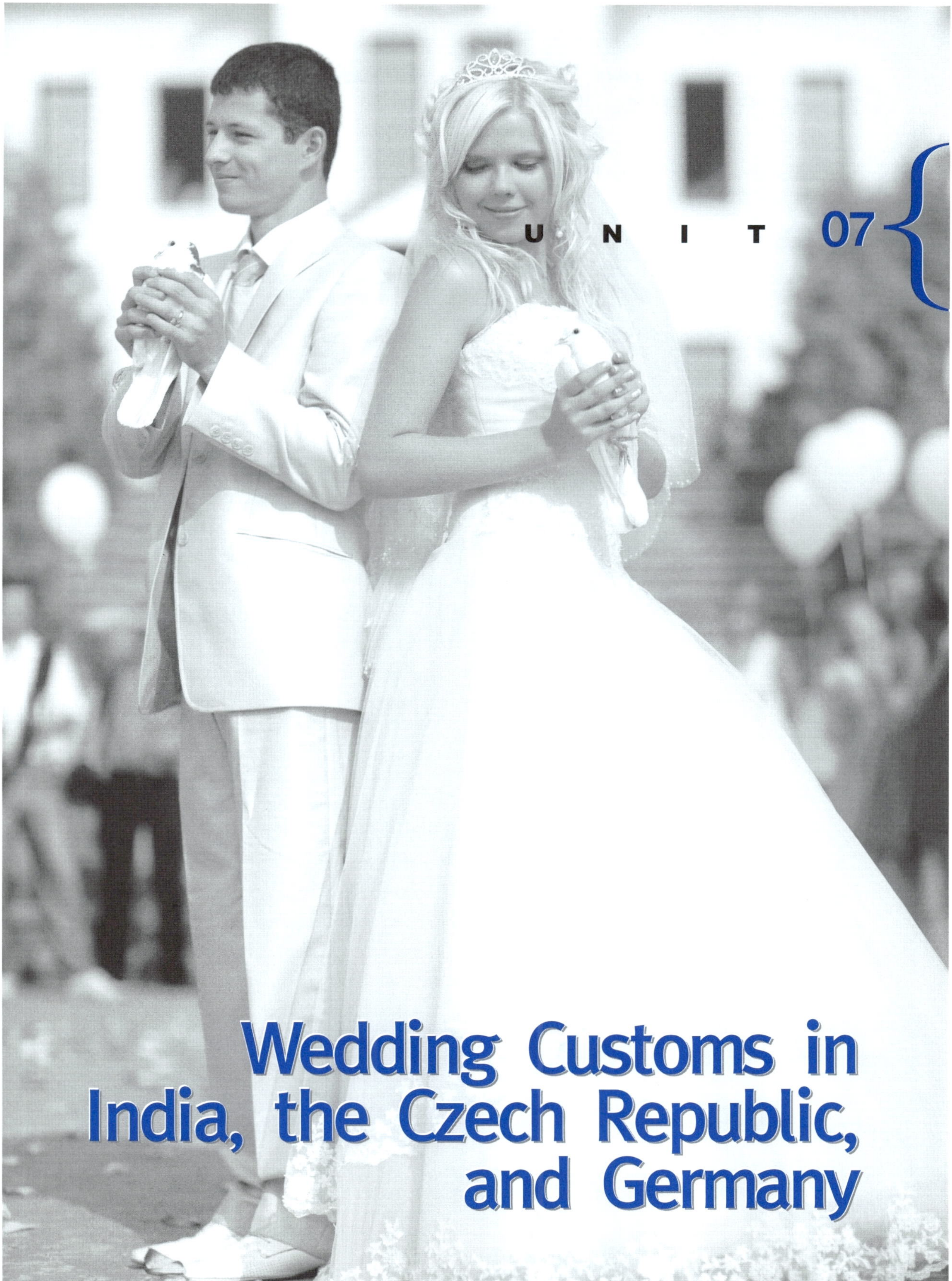

UNIT 07

Wedding Customs in India, the Czech Republic, and Germany

TOPIC READING

Read about Wedding Customs in India, the Czech Republic, and Germany.

Indian Wedding Celebrations

In India, weddings **are surrounded by** rituals and ceremonies. As part of the pre-wedding ceremonies, there is an engagement ceremony where the bride and groom exchange rings, and the families exchange gifts and sweets. Before the wedding ceremony, the bride's palms, wrists, arms, legs, and feet are decorated. On the wedding day, the bride and groom put flower garlands around each other's neck to show the bride has accepted the groom as her husband.

Wedding Ceremonies in the Czech Republic

Before the wedding, the bride's friends traditionally plant a tree in her yard and decorate the tree with colored ribbons and painted eggshells. According to the the Czech wedding ceremony. Before the marriage vows, a baby is placed in the couple's bed **in order to** bless their fertility. During the wedding ceremony, Czech women surround the bride dancing and singing. Then, they remove her veil and put on a handmade babushka.

German Wedding Ceremonies

German wedding tradition begins at birth. When a little girl is born in Germany, several trees are planted and these trees are sold once her wedding date is set. The money from the sale **is supposed to** be used for her marriage. Friends and family of the couple also create a wedding newspaper which **is filled with** pictures, articles and stories of the engaged couple. The proceeds from the newspaper, which is sold at the wedding, help **pay for** the honeymoon. The marriage ceremony has three parts. First, there is the day when couples have a civil ceremony at the city hall. The next night is the party where many friends and neighbors bring old dishes to break, believing it to be good luck. The third day is the religious ceremony. The flower girl, the bride's only attendant, walks in front of the bride and sprinkles petals on the floor to wish the couple good luck.

READING COMPREHENSION

Answer the questions based on the story above.

1. In India, what do they do for an engagement ceremony?

___

___

2. In Czech, why do they place a baby in the couple's bed?

___

___

3. In Germany, why do the friends and neighbors bring old dishes to break?

___

___

4. What is the wedding ceremony like in your country?

___

___

5. If you get married to a foreigner, what kind of wedding do you wish to have?

___

___

KEY EXPRESSIONS

Write the sentences in English using the words or phrases given.

1. be surrounded by

   ex) In India, weddings are surrounded by rituals and ceremonies.

   1) ______________________________

   2) ______________________________

2. in order to

   ex) Before the marriage vows, a baby is placed in the couple's bed in order to bless their fertility.

   1) ______________________________

   2) ______________________________

3. be supposed to

   ex) The money from the sale is supposed to be used for her marriage.

   1) ______________________________

   2) ______________________________

4. be filled with

   ex) Friends and family of the couple also create a wedding newspaper which is filled with pictures, articles, and stories of the engaged couple.

   1) ______________________________

   2) ______________________________

5. pay for

   ex) The proceeds from the newspaper, which is sold at the wedding, help pay for the honeymoon.

   1) ______________________________

   2) ______________________________

MAKING SENTENCES

Unscramble the words to make the sentences.

1. a lot of / The park / flowers and trees / is surround by

   The park ______________________________.

2. early / set up / in order to / I / my alarm clock / get up

   I ______________________________.

3. in this film / He / played an important role

   He ______________________________.

4. some beautiful flowers / The vase / is filled with

   The vase ______________________________.

5. pay for / How much / your bag / did you

   How much ______________________________?

6. possible / I / will try / as much as

   I ______________________________.

7. that blue bag / This red bag / more expensive than / is

   This red bag ______________________________.

8. the best / from the restaurant / tastes / of all / This dish

   This dish ______________________________.

9. her sister / Mary / faster than / swims

Mary ____.

10. during the holiday / More and more / are seeking / young people / to travel overseas

More and more ____.

GRAMMAR FOCUS

Choose the correct word form in parentheses.

1. Tax evasion is (more, the more, many) prevalent among self-employed professionals.

2. The coffee is (strong, stronger, the strongest) than it was yesterday.

3. Tom is probably (best, the better, the best) player on the team.

4. The man is (the fattest, as fat as, fatter) an elephant in the zoo.

5. Future generations will have to share a (greater, greatest, more great) burden to support the elderly.

6. Korea earns (more, many, much) golds in the Asiad than in the Olympics.

7. Fasten your seat belt (tight, as tighter, as tightly) as possible.

8. His fight is to probe into one of the nation's (worst, worse, bad) maritime accident.

9. The company excavated 14 percent (most, much, more) dirt than previously planned.

10. In his (late, later, latest) visit to the plant, he was accompanied by several high-ranking officials.

FURTHER PRACTICE

Choose the one word or phrase that best completes the sentence.

1. Between June 2013 and June 2014, a total of 19,167 medical doctors had reported figures ___________ than the actual amounts they had earned.
   a) the lowest b) the most low
   c) lower d) the lower

2. I think that the Asian Games are also ___________ the Olympics.
   a) as importantly as b) as important as
   c) as more important as d) as more importantly as

3. The copy machine works ___________ because it has been repaired.
   a) the most efficiently b) the most efficient
   c) more efficiently d) more efficient

4. Korean medalists in the upcoming Incheon Asian Games will get ___________ financial rewards from the state than those in the 2012 London Olympics.
   a) very smaller b) many smaller
   c) far smallest d) far smaller

5. He thinks that it is ___________ day of his whole life.
   a) the excitingest b) more exciting
   c) the most exciting d) the more exciting

6. The meeting will start at 7:00 a.m., one hour ___________ than previous ones.
   a) the earlier b) earlier
   c) the earliest d) the most earliest

7. She said "Cooking begins ___________ 4:30 a.m.".

a) as earlier than
b) as earlier as
c) as the eariest as
d) as early as

8. If you need ___________ information, please let me know.

a) the most
b) more
c) many
d) the more

9. The new smart phone is ___________ on the market.

a) the most expensivest
b) the most expensive
c) more expensive
d) the most expensively

10. My brother's English skill is ___________ mine.

a) better than
b) the best
c) the better than
d) better

UNIT 08

Wedding Customs in Islam, Jamaica, and Japan

TOPIC READING

Read about Wedding Customs in Islam, Jamaica, and Japan.

Islamic Wedding Ceremonies.

The traditional marriage is simple, however, many Muslims also hold multi-day celebrations **in honor of** the wedding. The bride and groom are separated at the wedding and can only see each other if their families allow them to. The officiant goes to each room and asks the bride and groom separately if they take each other in marriage. A marriage contract is then signed **in front of** witnesses. Once the contract is signed, the couple is brought together and declared husband and wife.

Jamaican Wedding Ceremonies

Jamaican weddings are community affairs, and the people in the village often come together to help plan the wedding. Everyone in the village also gathers in the street to see the bride and if she is not in tip-top shape, she is publicly criticized. While women wear a typical white wedding dress, men wear a bush jacket for the event. Married women wearing white dresses carry the confections to the wedding. The reception is often held at the groom's house, in a booth specially constructed for the event and **made of** coconut boughs and flowers. The wedding celebration also includes **an abundance of** dancing.

Japanese Wedding Ceremonies

Japanese ceremonies were traditionally held in Shinto Shrines. The bride is painted pure white **from** head **to** toe, declaring she is a maiden. She also wears a white kimono and an elaborate head piece. To symbolize their union, the couple drinks sake together, becoming husband and wife once they take the first sip. Brides have quite a few costume changes during the reception, first changing into a red kimono and then later into a Western-style dress.

READING COMPREHENSION

Answer the questions based on the story above.

1. In Islamic countries, what does an officiant do at the wedding?

____

____

2. What are the things you like and you do not like about the Jamaican wedding?

____

____

3. What do you think about the Japanese wedding?

____

____

4. Do you want a Korean traditional wedding? Why or why not?

____

____

5. Do you think having a wedding ceremony is important? Why or why not?

____

____

KEY EXPRESSIONS

Write the sentences in English using the words or phrases given.

1. in honor of

ex) The traditional marriage is simple, however, many Muslims also hold muti-day celebrations in honor of the wedding.

1) ____________________

2) ____________________

2. In front of

ex) A marriage contract is then signed in front of witnesses.

1) ____________________

2) ____________________

3. be made of

ex) The reception is often held at the groom's house, in a booth specially constructed for the event and made of coconut boughs and flowers.

1) ____________________

2) ____________________

4. an abundance of

ex) The wedding celebration also includes an abundance of dancing.

1) ____________________

2) ____________________

5. from A to B

ex) The bride is painted pure white from head to toe, declaring she is a maiden.

1) ____________________

2) ____________________

MAKING SENTENCES

Unscramble the words to make the sentences.

1. gold / The necklace / is made of / on my desk

   The necklace ____.

2. Though / in such good shape / getting older / she is / she is

   Though ____.

3. in honor of / the late teacher / was held / The event

   The event ____.

4. in front of / The woman / the door / is standing

   The woman ____.

5. animals and plants / There are / in the zoo / an abundance of

   There are ____.

6. for the exam / Last Sunday / from 3:00 p.m. to 7:00 p.m. / studied English / I

   Last Sunday, ____.

7. I was / skating / I / when / was poor at / young

   I ____.

8. as well / She / but also lonely / looks / not only happy

She ____.

9. by a car / the road / was almost run over / I was crossing / I / while

I ____.

10. was cancelled / rain / The event / because of

The event ____.

GRAMMAR FOCUS

Choose the correct word form in parentheses.

1. Her parents have supported her (despite, in spite, while) their financial burden.

2. He accumulated wealth by embezzling company funds (because, although, while) running firms.

3. Has the light on your modem been flashing ever (while, since, when) it stopped working?

4. (Due to, According to, In stead of) the bank, its balance of mortgage loans stood at 57.6 trillion won as of August, 28.

5. They looked forward to (celebrating, celebrate, be celebrating) the group's 10th anniversary next year.

6. It remains to be seen (since, whether, weather) the cell phone project will be continued after the testing period or not.

7. If (deploy, deploying, deployed), the primary purpose of the Terminal High Altitude Area Defence missile battery would be to defend its troops.

8. The policy priority of (either, both, neither) the central and municipal governments is economic revival.

9. (According to, Due to, Instead of) supplying homes massively in suburbs, it is better to increase supply downtown by promoting reconstruction.

10. Not only Seoul (but also, as well as, and) other municipalities, suffer from financial difficulties.

FURTHER PRACTICE

Choose the one word or phrase that best completes the sentence.

1. I feel good ___________ hearing compliments about my appearances.

   a) when b) although
   c) in spite of d) before

2. The upcoming nationwide safety inspections should deal with not only public facilities but ___________.

   a) practice regulation b) practices regulations
   c) practices regulation d) practice regulations

3. The governing party is entirely ___________ this idea.

   a) oppose to b) opposing to
   c) opposed of d) opposed to

4. She took her own life ___________ suffering from severe depression ___________ being sexually harassed.

   a) despite — after b) in spite of — before
   c) due to — after d) due to — before

5. He stole customer information from a company's website ___________ blackmailed the company.

   a) unless b) and
   c) or d) when

6. ___________ the beginning of this year, the North has tested rockets and missiles on 18 occasions.

   a) When b) Since
   c) While d) Though

7. Studies have shown that Internet addictions __________ adults has eased over time, __________ it is beginning to spiral out of control among young people.

a) among — while b) between — while
c) among — when d) between — when

8. Koreans rarely drink water out of the tap __________ because they think it is unsafe to drink __________ that it tastes bad.

a) either — and b) neither — nor
c) either — or d) either — nor

9. Monday's announcement came after a series of talks __________ the two ministries.

a) among b) between
c) either d) other

10. Two special Forces soldiers died while __________ on Tuesday.

a) training b) trained
c) train d) to train

Ready for
College English

UNIT 09

The Day of the Dead

TOPIC READING

Read about the Day of the Dead.

The Day of the Dead is a Mexican holiday. It is celebrated throughout Mexico and **around the world** in other cultures. The holiday **focuses on** the gathering of family and friends to pray for and remember friends and family members who have died. It is particularly celebrated in Mexico. The celebration takes place on October 31st, November 1st, and November 2nd, **in connection with** the triduum of All Hallows' Eve, All Saints' Day, and All Souls' Day.

The Day of the Dead celebrations in Mexico can **be traced back** to pre-Columbian. The festivities **were dedicated to** the goddess known as the "Lady of the Dead", corresponding to the modern Catrina. In most regions of Mexico, November 1 is to honor children and infants. Deceased adults are honored on November 2.

Day of the Dead, the three-day celebration, can be summarized as follows. On October 31st, All Hallows' Eve, the children make a children's altar to invite the spirits of dead children to come back for a visit. November 1st is All Saints' Day when the adult spirits come to visit. November 2nd is All Souls' Day, when families go to the cemetery to decorate the graves and tombs of their relatives. The three-day fiesta is filled with marigolds, sugar skulls, cardboard skeletons, fruit and nuts, incense, and other traditional foods and decorations.

READING COMPREHENSION

Answer the questions based on the story above.

1. What is Day of the Dead?

____

____

2. Who is All Hallows' Eve for?

____

____

3. Who is All Saints' Day for?

____

____

4. What do people do on All Souls' Day?

____

____

5. Do you have anything similar to Day of the Dead in your culture?

____

____

KEY EXPRESSIONS

Write the sentences in English using the words or phrases given.

1. around the world

ex) *It is celebrated throughout Mexico and around the world in other cultures.*

1) ______________________________

2) ______________________________

2. focus on

ex) *The holiday focuses on the gathering of family and friends.*

1) ______________________________

2) ______________________________

3. in connection with

ex) *The celebration takes place on October 31, November 1 and November 2, in connection with the triduum of All Hallow's Eve, Hallowmas itself, All Saint's Day, and All Soul's Day.*

1) ______________________________

2) ______________________________

4. trace back

ex) *The Day of the Dead celebrations in Mexico can be traced back to pre-Columbian.*

1) ______________________________

2) ______________________________

5. be dedicated to

ex) *The festivities were dedicated to the goddess known as the "Lady of the Dead".*

1) ______________________________

2) ______________________________

MAKING SENTENCES

Unscramble the words to make the sentences.

1. around the world / My husband / someday / I / and / want to travel

   My husband ____.

2. this morning / Why / your work / focus on / don't you

   Why ____?

3. to the 1980's / The problem / can be traced back

   The problem ____.

4. in connection with / There are / this subject / lots of problems

   There are ____.

5. for many years / He / fundraising for charities / has been dedicated to

   He ____.

6. are available / TOEIC / within two years / that is taken

   TOEIC ____.

7. who knew / to the question / few students / There were / an answer

   There were ____.

8. wearing / the red dress/ the woman / Who is

   Who is ____?

9. red and blue / bought / whose cover / I / the book / is

I ____.

10. whom / He / my English teacher / yesterday / I met / is

He ____.

GRAMMAR FOCUS

Choose the correct relative pronoun in parentheses.

1. She has her own family (whom, which, what) she celebrates the holiday with.

2. The birthrate was particularly low in Seoul's Jongno, (who, which, that) had an 0.729 birthrate.

3. Information and positions (who, that, whom) they offer should be provided in other languages.

4. I know the girl (who, that, whose) mother is my teacher.

5. The traffic accident prevention plan was one of the 25 key policy goals (who, which, whom) the municipal government announced in Thursday's four-year policy map.

6. Out of 62 companies (which, who, whom) participated in the event, only three provided their information in English.

7. Since 2011, 557 students have enrolled in the school (who, whom, which) she founded.

8. Most of executives (whom, who, which) get the warning used to quit their jobs.

9. The goods (which, whom, who) were delivered on May 2nd were seriously damaged.

10. I bought the book for (that, whose, which) I have been looking.

FURTHER PRACTICE

Choose the one word or phrase that best completes the sentence.

1. The president said that regulations ____________ private participation in markets should be revised.
   a) preventing　　b) prevented
   c) to prevent　　d) prevent

2. Women ____________ live in Seoul had an average 0.968 children in 2013, lower than the 1.187 national average.
   a) which　　b) who
   c) whom　　d) what

3. Defense officials say they are developing a low-tier missile shield ____________ called the Korea Air and missile defense system.
   a) who is　　b) whom is
   c) which are　　d) which is

4. For those ____________ have difficulty understanding Korean, 20 to 30 interpreters from 12 countries were deployed.
   a) who　　b) which
   c) whom　　d) what

5. The electronics maker is set to roll out strategic products ____________ it says will present a "better future" for consumers.
   a) who　　b) that
   c) whom　　d) what

6. I couldn't first believe the news ____________ I heard on the radio.
   a) that　　b) who
   c) whom　　d) what

7. You may refund full credit for any merchandise with ____________ you aren't satisfied.

a) that
b) which
c) whom
d) who

8. The student ____________ grades were high entered the prestigious university.

a) that
b) whose
c) which
d) who

9. Kim, ____________ is the former defender for his team and retired last year, has successfully developed his career as a commentator.

a) that
b) which
c) who
d) whom

10. Give apples to those ____________ you owe an apology to.

a) whom
b) who
c) whose
d) what

Ready for
College English

UNIT 10

The Mid-Autumn Festival

TOPIC READING

Read about the Mid-Autumn Festival.

The Mid-Autumn Festival is an official harvest festival celebrated by Chinese and Vietnamese people. The festival is held on the 15th day of the eighth month in the Chinese and Vietnamese calendar, during a full moon. It is in late September or early October on the Western calendar. The government of the People's Republic of China listed the festival as an "intangible cultural heritage" in 2006 and a public holiday in 2008. It is also a public holiday in Taiwan. Among the Vietnamese, it is considered the second-most important holiday. The festival is also **known by** other names such as the Moon Festival and Mooncake Festival.

Making and sharing mooncakes is **one of** the hallmark traditions of this festival. In Chinese culture, a round shape symbolizes completeness and unity. Thus, sharing round mooncakes among family members signifies the completeness and unity of families. In some areas of China, there is a tradition of making mooncakes during the night of the Mid-Autumn Festival. The senior member of the family would **cut** the mooncakes **into** pieces and distribute them to each family member, signifying a family reunion. These days, many people buy mooncakes **instead of** making them. One tradition is to pile 13 mooncakes **on top of** each other to mimic a pagoda. The number 13 represents the 13 months in a full lunar year.

READING COMPREHENSION

Answer the questions based on the story above.

1. What is the Mid-Autumn Festival?

____

____

2. What are other names for the Mid-Autumn Festival?

____

____

3. What does sharing mooncakes signify?

____

____

4. Do you have any similar tradition to Mid-Autumn Festival in your culture?

____

____

5. When your family members get together for traditional holidays, what subjects do you talk about?

____

____

KEY EXPRESSIONS

Write the sentences in English using the words or phrases given.

1. be known by

ex) *The festival is also known by other names such as the Moon Festival and the Moon Cake Festival.*

1) ______________________________

2) ______________________________

2. on of ~s

ex) *Making and sharing mooncakes is one of the hallmark traditions of the festival.*

1) ______________________________

2) ______________________________

3. cut A into B

ex) *The senior member of in the family would cut the mooncakes into pieces and distribute them to each family member, signifying family reunion.*

1) ______________________________

2) ______________________________

4. instead of

ex) *These days, many people buy mooncakes instead of making them.*

1) ______________________________

2) ______________________________

5. on top of

ex) *One tradition is to pile 13 mooncakes on top of each other to mimic a pagoda.*

1) ______________________________

2) ______________________________

MAKING SENTENCES

Unscramble the words to make the sentences.

1. at university / is / He / one of my friends

   He ____.

2. two pieces / peel an apple / Please / cut it into / and

   Please ____.

3. instead of / have a sandwich / a hamburger / Will you

   Will ____?

4. in Korea / that / is known by / his name / most people / I think

   I think ____.

5. the building / There are / on top of / lots of people

   There are ____.

6. your health / Playing tennis / for / may be good

   Playing ____.

7. the air conditioner / Would you / turning on / mind

   Would you ____?

8. stops running / on the weekend / The subway / at midnight

   The subway ____.

9. earlier / to become / He / the president / helped her

He ____.

10. this week / is scheduled to / He / to Europe / travel

He ____.

GRAMMAR FOCUS

Choose the correct word form in parentheses.

1. The app lets users (check, to check, checking) their running routes.

2. (To have, Have, Having) sports stars as commentators is nothing unusual for broadcasters.

3. The app also allows user (share, to share, sharing) all data generated through the app on social networking services.

4. To avoid (repeating, repeat, to repeat) the same mistakes, we need to approach regulatory reform in a different manner.

5. I plan (meet, to meet, meeting) as many people as possible and (listen to, listen, listening to) them.

6. My parents are going to America (to see, see, seeing) my brother.

7. The Prime Minister's Office should consider (to give, give, giving) the government organizations responsibility, authority, and incentive.

8. I am doing this by not just (giving, to give, give) them fish, but (teach, to teach, teaching) them how to fish.

9. She forgot (turning off, to turn off, turn off) the lights when she left the office.

10. We need to adopt a bold approach (improving, to improve, improve) the relations with Korea.

FURTHER PRACTICE

Choose the one word or phrase that best completes the sentence.

1. The government said Tuesday it has decided to allow public schools ____________ English to first and second graders during after school programs.
   a) teaching b) to teach
   c) teach d) to be taught

2. We started ____________ in the morning, but we haven't finished yet.
   a) to be work b) working
   c) work d) to be worked

3. The president has emphasized that deregulation is a significant part of her three-year plan ____________ the economy.
   a) boosting b) boost
   c) to be boosted d) to boost

4. She refused ____________ it until she gets an apology.
   a) returning b) to be return
   c) to return d) return

5. I will make the people ____________ the cultural enrichment in their lives.
   a) to feel b) feel
   c) feeing d) to be felt

6. Because child care and education are a big burden, couples delay ____________ a child or choose not to have one at all.
   a) having b) to have
   c) to be having d) have

7. University students, who borrowed money to pay for their tuition, could find it hard ____________ jobs because of their lower grades.

a) finding　　b) to find
c) to be found　　d) find

8. As I said at the hearing and told government employees, ____________ is the key.

a) listen careful　　b) listening careful
c) listen carefully　　d) listening carefully

9. It is difficult for students from low income brackets ____________ the vicious cycle of poverty.

a) to break out　　b) break out
c) breaking out　　d) to be broke out

10. Broadcasters will stop ____________ analog TV signals by Dec 31, 2012.

a) transplanting　　b) transmitting
c) transpiring　　d) transmit

Ready for
College English

UNIT 11

Fascinating Funeral Traditions

TOPIC READING

Read about Fascinating Funeral Traditions around the Globe.

The New Orleans Jazz Funeral

It is one of the common images of New Orleans, Louisiana: the noisy, jazz-tinged funeral procession. Funerals in New Orleans have a unique balance **between** joy **and** grief as mourners are lead by a marching band. The funerals are influenced by West African, French and African-American traditions. The band plays sorrowful music **at first**, but once the body is buried, they shift to an upbeat note. Cathartic dancing is generally **a part of** the event, to commemorate the life of the dead.

Philippine Death Traditions

Many ethnic groups in the Philippines have unique funeral practices. The people in Benguet of Northwestern Philippines blindfold the dead and place them **next to** the main entrance of the house. Tinguian people dress the dead in their best clothes, seat them on a chair and **place** a lit cigarette **in** their lips. Caviteno people, who live near Manila, bury the dead in a hollowed-out tree trunk. When someone becomes sick, they select the tree for burial. Apayo people, who live in the north, bury the dead under the kitchen.

READING COMPREHENSION

Answer the questions based on the story above.

1. What are the characteristics of funerals in New Orleans?

____

____

2. What do you think about death traditions in the Philippines?

____

____

3. What kind of funerals do you have in your culture?

____

____

4. What kind of funerals do you want when you die?

____

____

5. Do you think that funerals can be happy? Why or why not?

____

____

KEY EXPRESSIONS

Write the sentences in English using the words or phrases given.

1. between A and B

ex) *Funerals in New Orleans have a unique balance between joy and grief as mourners are lead by a marching band.*

1) ______________________________

2) ______________________________

2. at first

ex) *The band plays sorrowful music at first, but once the body is buried, they shift to an upbeat note.*

1) ______________________________

2) ______________________________

3. a part of

ex) *Cathartic dancing is generally a part of the event, to commemorate the life of the deceased.*

1) ______________________________

2) ______________________________

4. next to

ex) *The people blindfold the dead and place them next to the main entrance of the house.*

1) ______________________________

2) ______________________________

5. place A in B

ex) *Tinguian people dress the dead in their best clothes, seat them on a chair and place a lit cigarette in their lips.*

1) ______________________________

2) ______________________________

MAKING SENTENCES

Unscramble the words to make the sentences.

1. At first / told a lie / thought / I / she

   At first ____.

2. the reading club / He's / in his school / a part of

   He's ____.

3. the bank / The book store / just next to / is

   The book store ____.

4. some differences / between men / There are / and women

   There are ____.

5. your valuables / You should / in this safe / place

   You ____.

6. last night / were invited / My husband / to the party / and I

   My husband ____.

7. Korean food / in this restaurant / What kind of / is served

   What kind of ____?

8. by next Sunday / The frozen food / to the restaurant / must be delivered

   The frozen food ____.

9. going shopping / I / with my friend / am interested in

I ____.

10. the room / was broken / when / The door / came out of / she

The door ____.

GRAMMAR FOCUS

Choose the correct word form in parentheses.

1. The deregulation (was followed, followed, are followed) by the key rate cut.

2. The measure (increase, is increased, increased) mortgage loans.

3. A top presidential security aide (is expected by, is expected to, expected to) visit Washington this month.

4. Only a few civic groups (has been allowed to, have been allowed to, have been allowed by) visit and provide humanitarian aid.

5. The dispatched workers (are hired, hired, was hired) and (send, sent, sending) by contractors for specific types of jobs.

6. Parents will be (encouraged by, encouraged to, encourage to) set online gaming curfews for their children.

7. English education is so important that it needs to (teaching, be teaching, be taught) as early as possible.

8. A 39-year-old Nigerian man (quarantined, were quarantined, was quarantined) after being diagnosed with a high fever.

9. The insurance company (covers, is covered, cover) everything including the damage of the shipment.

10. It is a general rule of thumb (to not be involved in, not to be involved in, not to be involved by) other people's business.

FURTHER PRACTICE

Choose the one word or phrase that best completes the sentence.

1. Kim's leg was broken; Lee's finger ___________; Park's wrist ___________.

   a) was burnt — was sprained　　b) burned — sprained
   c) is burnt — is sprained　　d) burn — sprain

2. Because it ___________, the copy machine works more efficiently.

   a) have been repaired　　b) has repaired
   c) has been repaired　　d) has been repairing

3. The building was not ___________ well and will ___________ soon.

   a) construct — collapse　　b) constructed — collapsed
   c) constructed — collapse　　d) construct — collapsed

4. These two English words 'hour and our' have the same pronunciation although they ___________ differently.

   a) spelled　　b) are spelt
   c) are spelled　　d) were spelled

5. Speaking, reading, and writing English ___________ by training.

   a) can improve　　b) can be improved
   c) can be improving　　d) can be improve

6. Kim usually ___________ to school by bicycle but today he ___________ by subway due to heavy rain.

   a) goes — went　　b) goes — goes
   c) is gone — went　　d) is gone — was gone

7. He ____________ a Korean-American mother, and an American father, and ____________ with a son.

a) was born to — married to
b) was born to — married with
c) is born to — married to
d) was born with — married with

8. Seoul Central District Court ____________ her to a three-year-prison term for embezzling company's money.

a) was sentenced
b) sentence
c) sentenced
d) is sentenced

9. The university ____________ its student a well-rounded education.

a) give
b) is given
c) gives
d) is being given

10. The theater at the corner ____________ people who love movies.

a) is filled with
b) is filled by
c) is filled
d) is filled in

UNIT 12

Ice Bucket Challenge

TOPIC READING

Read about the Ice Bucket Challenge.

The Ice Bucket Challenge, sometimes called the ALS Ice Bucket Challenge, was an activity involving dumping a bucket of ice water on someone's head. The purpose of this was to promote awareness of the disease, amyotrophic lateral sclerosis(ALS) and encourage donations to research. It **went viral** on social media in July and August, 2014. In the U.S., many people participated for the ALS Association, and in the U.K., many people participated for the Motor Neuron Disease Association. Some people have **opted to** donate their money from the Ice bucket challenge to other organizations.

These are the rules. Within 24 hours of being challenged, participants have to record a video of themselves in continuous footage. First, they are to announce their acceptance of the challenge **followed by** pouring ice into a bucket of water. Second, the bucket is to be lifted and poured over the participant's head. Third, the participant can **call out** a challenge to other people. Whether people choose to donate, perform the challenge, or do both varies. In one version of the challenge, the participant **is expected to** donate $10 if they have poured the ice water over their head or donate $100 if they have not. Some individual videos have included the participants saying that they will be making a donation along with performing the challenge.

READING COMPREHENSION

Answer the questions based on the story above.

1. What is the Ice Bucket Challenge for?

____

____

2. What are the rules of the Ice Bucket Challenge?

____

____

3. What do you think about the idea of the Ice Bucket Challenge?

____

____

4. Do you want to participate in the Ice Bucket Challenge? Why or why not?

____

____

5. Can you think of other good ideas to help sick people?

____

____

KEY EXPRESSIONS

Write the sentences in English using the words or phrases given.

1. go viral

    ex) *It went viral on social media during July and August 2014.*

    1) ______________________________

    2) ______________________________

2. opt to

    ex) *Some people have opted to donate their money from the Ice Bucket Challenge to other organizations.*

    1) ______________________________

    2) ______________________________

3. be followed by

    ex) *First, they are to announce their acceptance of the challenge followed by pouring ice into a bucket of water.*

    1) ______________________________

    2) ______________________________

4. call out

    ex) *Third, the participant can call out a challenge to other people.*

    1) ______________________________

    2) ______________________________

5. be expected to

    ex) *In one version of the challenge, the participant is expected to donate $10 if they have poured the ice water over their head or donate $100 if they have not.*

    1) ______________________________

    2) ______________________________

MAKING SENTENCES

Unscramble the words to make the sentences.

1. has been gone viral / Recently / in the market / the smart phone

   Recently, ____.

2. to America / young people / A number of / opt to emigrate

   A number of ____.

3. are expected to / After the summit / the two leaders / a joint statement / adopt

   After the summit, ____.

4. a question and answer session / His speech / will be followed by

   His speech ____.

5. until / call out / Please wait here / your name / I

   Please wait here ____.

6. some cookies / If / a convenience store, / you pass / get me

   If ____.

7. I could buy / more money, / I had / a nice car / If

   If ____.

8. with my family / I wish / go abroad / I could

I ____.

9. couldn't have done / Without his help, / by then / I / it

Without his help, ____________________________________.

10. everything / She speaks / she knew / as if

She speaks ____.

GRAMMAR FOCUS

Choose the correct word form in parentheses.

1. If I (studied harder, study harder, have studied harder), I could pass the exam.

2. One in three smokers said they will quit if the health ministry (will raise, raises, raise) cigarette prices as planned.

3. I felt as if the sky (has fallen down, fall down, had fallen down) when I heard the news.

4. I hope I (will, would, can) get a higher score on TOEIC test this time.

5. (Had it not been, Has it not been, If it has not been) for heavy snow, she could have arrived there on time.

6. If we make a sincere effort to create an atmosphere favorable for dialogue, North Korea (finally responds, will finally respond, finally respond) and cooperate.

7. He would face more than one year, to life in prison, for taking bribes if he is (found, had found, has found) guilty.

8. You will miss the train because of heavy traffic (if, unless, if not) you leave the office right now.

9. You should apologize to me for doing so; (but, although, otherwise), I will take legal action against you.

10. I wouldn't keep on making the same mistakes over and over again if I (was, are, were) you.

FURTHER PRACTICE

Choose the one word or phrase that best completes the sentence.

1. If a war ____________, it will be more difficult to preemptively counteract the North's attack.
   a) breaks out   b) will break out
   c) break out   d) broke out

2. It is nearly impossible to find flight tickets to overseas destinations unless you ____________ the tickets early.
   a) don't buy   b) didn't buy
   c) buy   d) bought

3. ____________ the internet, we wouldn't get enough information from all over the world through the internet.
   a) If   b) But for
   c) With   d) Through

4. ____________ it was easier for foreigners to report illegal activities without fear of being fired, deported, or arrested.
   a) I want   b) I wish
   c) I hope   d) I like

5. If he had gone to America five years ago, he ____________ here with me now.
   a) wouldn't be   b) wouldn't have been
   c) would be   d) would have been

6. I would go abroad to study a foreign language if I ____________ a lottery.
   a) win   b) had won
   c) has won   d) won

7. He would be sentenced to 20 years ___________.

a) if he convicted
b) if he had been convicted
c) if convicted
d) if he convicts

8. ___________ that more carefully, I wouldn't have made these silly mistakes.

a) If I looked into
b) If you should look into
c) If I have looked into
d) Had I looked into

9. You look as if you ___________ since you are wearing high heels.

a) have long legs
b) had long legs
c) had had long legs
d) have had long legs

10. ___________, you would do the same thing I did.

a) Was you a parent
b) Were you a parent
c) If you was a parent
d) If you are a parent

Ready for
College English

Answer Key

UNIT 01 Potluck

Unscramble the words to make each sentence.

1. Jeju Island is referred to as one of the most popular places in the world.
2. I am going shopping with my friend this Friday.
3. Where does our English teacher come from?
4. He goes to movies with his wife once every three months.
5. She happened to meet her friend on her way to school.
6. After they collected money, they counted it.
7. The temperatures in summer range from 30℃ to 35℃ in Seoul.
8. The sales person admitted that it was his fault.
9. We sometimes use body language when we communicate with each other.
10. I don't want to be associated with those kinds of people.

Choose the correct noun in parentheses.

1. The man 2. an American 3. manager 4. a flower 5. three 6. the man 7. a cup of coffee 8. many customs 9. a surprising announcement 10. an English teacher

Choose the one word or phrase that best completes the sentence.

1. c) All participants 2. b) some information 3. a) speech 4. d) an-a 5. c) e-mails 6. b) whether to attend 7. c) patience 8. a) books 9. b) The furniture 10. a) a scientist

UNIT 02 Black Friday

Unscramble the words to make each sentence.

1. This smart phone is regarded as one of the best ones on the market.
2. The Incheon Asian Games kicked off on Sept, 19.
3. My opinion is similar to yours.
4. In lieu of jail term, Tom is sentenced to community service.
5. I like fruits such as apples, oranges, and bananas.
6. Some students in my class are from rural areas.
7. How long have you been in this city?
8. He told me that he had already finished his homework.
9. Most people are sitting on the bench in the park.
10. Can I have your name and phone number please?

Choose the correct pronoun in parentheses.

1. mine 2. herself 3. hers 4. one-the other 5. themselves 6. me 7. our 8. me-they 9. They-his 10. hers-mine

Choose the one word or phrase that best completes the sentence.

1. b) Mary and her sister 2. b) you and he 3. c) mine 4. b) those 5. b) Not everyone 6. d) ones 7. a) that 8. b) It is 9. a) one 10. c) others

UNIT 03 Baby Showers

Unscramble the words to make each sentence.

1. A variety of goods are displayed in the store.
2. The roofs of the temples are round.
3. Many people are having their meals and talking in the restaurant.
4. It is important to study English hard to get a good job.
5. Who took your mother to the hospital yesterday?
6. The woman is wearing a short sleeved shirt.
7. The event will be held at the school next month.
8. I am speaking on behalf of my family.
9. It is impossible for us to solve the problem in five minutes.
10. According to the newspaper, three people were killed in the accident.

Choose the correct verb form and tense in parentheses.

1. plays 2. studied 3. was waiting 4. work 5. heard 6. have been 7. graduated 8. had already left 9. hear 10. was walking-saw

Choose the one word or phrase that best completes the sentence.

1. a) goes-is going 2. d) attempted 3. c) has called 4. b) will run 5. a) have been deported 6. a) is preparing 7. d) have passed 8. b) finishes 9. c) had seen 10. b) teach

UNIT 04 La Tomatina

Unscramble the words to make each sentence.

1. I wouldn't like to get involved in it.
2. You should take responsibility for the death of him.
3. The police forced him to tell the truth about the accident.
4. She allows her children to watch educational programs.
5. People go through many difficult times in their lives.
6. You can return faulty products anytime.
7. The dish was so hot that I couldn't eat it.
8. My sister went to school late because she was sick.
9. I didn't find anything interesting in your essay.
10. My mother-in-law cooks food very well.

Circle the subject and choose the correct verb form to complete each sentence.

1. is 2. are 3. are 4. are 5. is 6. chair 7. are 8. likes 9. are 10. is

Choose the one word or phrase that best completes the sentence.

1. a) enjoy 2. b) are chinese 3. d) have been improved 4. c) are affecting 5. b) am going 6. b) is 7. a) are adopting 8. d) drove 9. a) are not 10. a) were not any

UNIT 05 The Water Festival

Unscramble the words to make each sentence.

1. She is looking at a sleeping baby in her room.
2. He has already thrown away the broken window.
3. Unfortunately, he ended up failing the test.
4. My sister and I are so different from one another.
5. He put on a black suit and rushed out of the house.
6. FTA will take effect at the beginning of this year.
7. The movie was boring and I was bored.
8. I have the letter typed by my secretary.
9. Some applicants are nervous waiting for the job interview.
10. I gave the returned item to the clerk.

Choose the correct adjective or adverb in parentheses.

1. perfectly 2. healthy 3. good 4. well-good 5. beautiful 6. loudly 7. Few 8. highly likely 9. much 10. happy

Choose the one word or phrase that best completes the sentence.

1. b) important 2. a) likely 3. b) strategic 4. c) advisable-carefully 5. c) directly 6. a) environmentally-friendly 7. c) Nearly 8. b) eligible-electronically 9. c) sad 10. b) considerable

UNIT 06 Valentine's Day

Unscramble the words to make each sentence.

1. Please contact us if you have any questions or comments.
2. Why don't we go out for dinner sometime next week?
3. They met, fell in love, and married last year.
4. Every student likes the class very much.
5. Valentine's Day is known as a time of love.
6. The goal of this course is to provide you with practical experience.
7. The man was known as an actor, not a singer.
8. A number of students are waiting for their teacher in the classroom.
9. The man is looking for something in the box.
10. He was portrayed as a monster in the film.

Choose the correct participle in parentheses.

1. Retired 2. advanced 3. contrasting 4. developing 5. arriving 6. organizing 7. working-level 8. following 9. secured 10. deteriorating

Choose the one word or phrase that best completes the sentence.

1. b) charged 2. a) growing 3. d) training 4. c) honoring 5. a) changed 6. b) restricted 7. c) fundraising 8. b) escalating 9. a) proposed 10. a) impressed-impressing

UNIT 07 Wedding Customs in India, the Czech Republic, and Germany

Unscramble the words to make each sentence.

1. The park is surrounded by a lot of flowers and trees.
2. I set up my alarm clock in order to get up early.
3. He played an important role in this film.
4. The vase is filled with some beautiful flowers.
5. How much did you pay for your bag?
6. I will try as much as possible.
7. This red bag is more expensive than that blue bag.
8. This dish from the restaurant tastes the best of all.
9. Mary swims faster than Mary's sister.
10. More and more young people are seeking to travel overseas during the holiday.

Choose the correct word form in parentheses.

1. more 2. stronger 3. the best 4. as fat as 5. greater 6. more 7. as tightly 8. worst 9. more 10. latest

Choose the one word or phrase that best completes the sentence.

1. c) lower 2. b) as important as 3. c) more efficiently 4. d) far smaller 5. c) the most exciting 6. b) earlier 7. d) as early as 8. b) more 9. b) the most expensive 10. a) better than

UNIT 08 Wedding Customs in Islam, Jamaica, and Japan

Unscramble the words to make each sentence.

1. The necklace on my desk is made of gold.
2. Though she is getting older, she is in such good shape.
3. The event was held in honor of the late teacher.
4. The woman is standing in front of the door.
5. There are an abundance of animals and plants in the zoo.
6. Last Sunday, I studied English for the exam from 3:00 p.m. to 7:00 p.m.
7. I was poor at skating when I was young.
8. She looks not only happy but also lonely as well.
9. I was almost run over by a car while I was crossing the road.
10. The event was cancelled because of rain.

Choose the correct conjunction or preposition in parentheses.

1. despite 2. while 3. since 4. According to 5. celebrating 6. whether 7. deployed 8. both 9. Instead of 10. but also

Choose the one word or phrase the best completes the sentence.

1. a) when 2. d) practice regulations 3. b) oppose to 4. c) due to-after 5. b) and 6. b) Since 7. a)among-while 8. c) either-or 9. b) between 10. a) training

UNIT 09 The Day of the Dead

Unscramble the words to make each sentence.

1. My husband and I want to travel around the world someday.
2. Why don't you focus on your work this morning?
3. The problem can be traced back to the 1980's.
4. There are lots of problems in connection with this subject.
5. He has been dedicated to fundraising for charities for many years.
6. TOEIC that is taken within two years are available.
7. There were few students who knew an answer to the question.
8. Who is the woman wearing the red dress?
9. I bought the book whose cover is red and blue.
10. He is my English teacher whom I met yesterday.

Choose the correct relative pronoun in parentheses.

1. whom 2. which 3. that 4. whose 5. which 6. which 7. which 8. who 9. which 10. which

Choose the one word or phrase that best completes the sentence.

1. a) preventing 2. b) who 3. d) which is 4. a) who 5. b) that 6. d) what 7. b) which 8. b) whose 9. c) who 10. a) whom

UNIT 10 The Mid-Autumn Festival

Unscramble the words to make each sentence.

1. He is one of my friends at university.
2. Please peel an apple and cut it into two pieces.
3. Will you have a sandwich instead of a hamburger?
4. I think that his name is known by most people in Korea.
5. There are lots of people on top of the building.
6. Playing tennis may be good for your health.
7. Would you mind turning on the air conditioner?
8. The subway stops running at midnight on weekend.
9. He helped her to become the president earlier.
10. He is scheduled to travel to Europe this week.

Choose the correct word form in parentheses.

1. check 2. Having 3. to share 4. repeating 5. to meet 6. to see 7. giving 8. giving-teaching 9. to turn off 10. to improve

Choose the one word or phrase that best completes the sentence.

1. b) to teach 2. b) working 3. d) to boost 4. c) to return 5. b) feel 6. a) having 7. b) to find 8. d) listening carefully 9. a) to break out 10. b) transmitting

UNIT 11 Fascinating Funeral Traditions

Unscramble the words to make each sentence.

1. At first I thought she told a lie.
2. He's a part of the reading club in his school.
3. The book store is just next to the bank.
4. There are some differences between men and women.
5. You should place your valuables in this safe.
6. My husband and I were invited to the party last night.
7. What kind of Korean food is served in this restaurant?
8. The frozen food must be delivered to the restaurant by next Sunday.
9. I am interested in going shopping with my friend.
10. The door was broken when she came out of the room.

Choose the correct word form in parentheses.

1. was followed 2. increased 3. is expected 4. have been allowed 5. are hired 6. will be encouraged to 7. be taught 8. was quarantined 9. covers 10. not to be involved

Choose the one word or phrase that best completes the sentence.

1. a) was burnt-was sprained 2. c) has been repaired 3. b) constructed-collapsed 4. c) are spelled 5. b) can be improved 6. a) goes-went 7. b) was born to-married with 8. c) sentenced 9. c) gives 10. a) is filled with

UNIT 12 Ice Bucket Challenge

Unscramble the words to make each sentence.

1. Recently, the smart phone has been gone viral in the market.
2. A number of young people opt to emigrate to America.
3. After the summit, the two leaders are expected to adopt a joint statement.
4. His speech will be followed by a question and answer session.
5. Please wait here until I call out your name.
6. If you pass a convenience store, get me some cookies.

7. If I had more money, I could buy a nice car.
8. I wish I could go abroad with my family.
9. Without his help, I couldn't have done it by then.
10. She speaks as if she knew everything.

Choose the correct word form in parentheses.

1. studied harder 2. raises 3. had fallen down 4. would 5. Had it not been 6. will finally respond 7. found 8. unless 9. otherwise 10. were

Choose the one word or phrase that best completes the sentence.

1. a) breaks out 2. c) buy 3. b) But for 4. b) I wish 5. a) wouldn't be 6. d) won 7. c) if convicted 8. d) Had I looked into 9. b) had long legs 10. b) Were you a parent

References

최이령(2010). 토마토 Grammaring, Seoul: Neungyule Education, Inc.

Anne Taylor & Garrett Byrne(2007). Very Easy TOEIC. Seoul. Compass Publishing.

Christopher Thompson(2007). The Best TOEIC. Seoul: Moonjinmedia Co. Ltd.

Hyejin Chung(2001). Starter TOEIC. Compass Publishing.

Jiyoung Nam(2010). Basic in Structure for TOEIC 1. Seoul: Brain House.

http://en.wikipedia.org/wiki/potluck Retrieved Sept, 2014.

http://en.wikipedia.org/wiki/Black_Friday_(shopping) Retrieved Sept, 2014.

http://en.wikipedia.org/wiki/water_festival Retrieved Sept, 2014.

http://en.wikipedia.org/wiki/La_Tomatina Retrieved Sept, 2014.

http://en.wikipedia.org/wiki/Baby_shower Retrieved Oct, 2014.

http://en.wikipedia.org/wiki/Valentine's_Day Retrieved Dec, 2014.

http://www.timeanddate.com/holidays/us/valentine-day Retrieved Dec, 2014.

http://www.businessinsider.com/how-weddings-are-celebrated-around-the-world-2011-10?op=1 Retrieved Oct, 2014.

http://www.businessinsider.com/how-weddings-are-celebrated-around-the-world-2011-10?op=1 Retrieved Oct, 2014.

http://en.wikipedia.org/wiki/day_of_the_dead Retrieved Nov, 2014.

http://en.wikipedia.org/wiki/Mid-Autumn_Festival Retrieved Nov, 2014.

http://blog.ted.com/2013/10/01/11-fascinating-funeral-traditions-from-around-the-globe/ Retrieved Nov, 2014.

http://en.wikipedia.org/wiki/Ice_Bucket_Challenge Retrieved Nov, 2014.

Ready for
College English